My Book About Food

This colourful book uses bold, bright photographs and simple words to help young children understand more about the food they eat. It describes the different kinds of food – meat, vegetables, fruit, cereals, milk and eggs – and explains that we need food to give us energy and keep us healthy. The book also looks at food production, shopping, cooking, meal times and food around the world. The words and pictures are designed to develop reading skills and promote interest and discussion.

My Book About

The Body · Houses and Homes
Clothes · Toys
Food · Weather

Editor: Anna Girling
Designer: Loraine Hayes

First published in 1991 by
Wayland (Publishers) Ltd
61 Western Road, Hove
East Sussex BN3 1JD, England

British Library Cataloguing in Publication Data
Jackman, Wayne
Food. – (My book about)
I. Title II. Series
428.4

ISBN 0 7502 0123 1

Typeset by Kalligraphic Design Ltd, Horley, Surrey
Printed and bound by Casterman S.A., Belgium

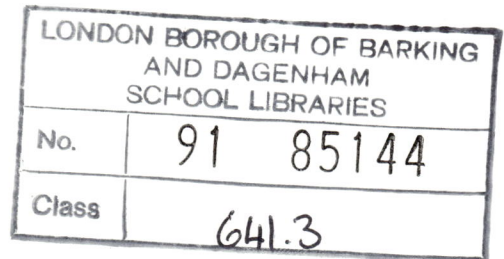

Words that are **underlined** in the text
are explained in the glossary on page 22.

My Book About Food

WAYNE JACKMAN

Wayland

Food gives us **energy** to work and play.
Look at this pile of tasty food.

Which of these foods do you like to eat?
Can you see the fish?

Food also keeps us **healthy**.
This girl is eating a sandwich. Lettuce and tomatoes taste nice with brown bread.

Do you think her sandwich is healthy?

There are many sorts of food. This is a field of **wheat**. The wheat is being cut by a big machine.

Do you know that bread is made from wheat?

6

Some food comes from animals.
Meat, milk and eggs all come from animals.

Most of our milk comes from cows.
Have you seen cows like these on a farm?

Lettuces are **vegetables**.
These lettuces look very green.

How many lettuces do you think there are in this big field?

We get our eggs from hens.

What noise does a hen make?

Most people buy their food in shops or at **markets**.
This market has lots of **fruit**.

What kinds of fruit can you see?

Sometimes people grow their own food.

This girl is helping to pick vegetables from the garden. **Can you see where she has put them?**

This boy wants to help with the **cooking**.
He is washing his hands.

Why must he have clean hands?

This boy is making a cake.
He has made a cake mix with eggs, milk and **flour**.

He is going to mix it all up.

Do you sit at a table to eat your meals?

This table is laid for **breakfast**.
What do you eat at breakfast time?

Look at all this food set out for a big meal. It is all **vegetarian** food.

Vegetarian food does not have meat in it.

These slices of pizza look good to eat. People all around the world eat pizza.

Do you know where it first came from?
It came from Italy.

Are your school lunches like this?

This girl in China is eating with **chopsticks**.
Eating with chopsticks can be hard at first!

We eat
different food
in **summer**
and **winter**.

This girl is eating
a **watermelon**.
**Do you think
it is summer
or winter?**
Perhaps her
sunglasses
help you guess.

A hot potato is good to eat when the weather is cold.

This girl is eating a hot baked potato outside.

Some food is great fun to eat.
Ice cream is **sweet** and tastes nice.
Too many sweet foods can be bad for you.

What kind of ice cream do you like best?

This girl is brushing her teeth to keep them healthy. Perhaps she has just eaten some sweet ice cream!

How many times do you brush your teeth every day?

Glossary

Breakfast The first meal of the day.

Chopsticks Two small sticks used to pick up food.

Cooking Getting food ready to eat by heating it.

Energy The strength to move and do things.

Flour A powder made from wheat and used for making bread, pastry and cakes.

Fruit The part of a plant that grows around the seeds and is good to eat.

Healthy Fit and well, not ill.

Markets Places where people sell food and other goods. They are usually outdoors.

Summer The time of year when the weather is warmest.

Sweet Tasting of sugar or honey.

Vegetables The parts of plants that are eaten as food.

Vegetarian Not having any meat. Vegetarians are people who do not eat meat and live mainly on vegetable food.

Watermelon A large fruit with a green skin and a pink, watery inside.

Wheat A plant grown for its seed, which is made into flour.

Winter The time of year when the weather is coldest.

Books to read

Food by Terry Jennings (Oxford University Press, 1984)

Food (A to Z series) by Beverley Mathias and Ruth Thomson (Franklin Watts, 1988)

Healthy Eating by Wayne Jackman (Wayland, 1990)

Let's Visit a Farm series by Sarah Doughty and Diana Bentley (Wayland, 1989–90)

My First Cookery Book by Wayne Jackman (Firefly, 1990)

Taste by Wayne Jackman (Wayland, 1990)

Picture acknowledgements

The publishers would like to thank the following for providing the photographs for this book: Tony Stone Worldwide 7, 8, 9 (Michael Kornafel), 11 (Ron Sutherland), 15 (Robin Smith); Wayland Picture Library 12 (Trevor Hill), 14 (Trevor Hill), 17, 19 (Trevor Hill); Timothy Woodcock 5, 13; Zefa cover 4, 6, 10, 16, 18, 20 (N. Schafer), 21.

Index